dinosaurs
on my street

David West

FIREFLY BOOKS

A Firefly Book

Published by Firefly Books Ltd. 2013

Second printing

Publisher Cataloging-in-Publication Data (U.S.)

A CIP record for this title is available from the Library of Congress

Library and Archives Canada Cataloguing in Publication

A CIP record for this title is available from Library and Archives Canada

Published in the United States by
Firefly Books (U.S.) Inc.
P.O. Box 1338, Ellicott Station
Buffalo, New York 14205

Published in Canada by
Firefly Books Ltd.
50 Staples Avenue, Unit 1
Richmond Hill, Ontario L4B 0A7

Printed in the United States of America

Conceived, designed and produced by
David West Children's Books
7 Princeton Court, 55 Felsham Road,
London SW15 1AZ

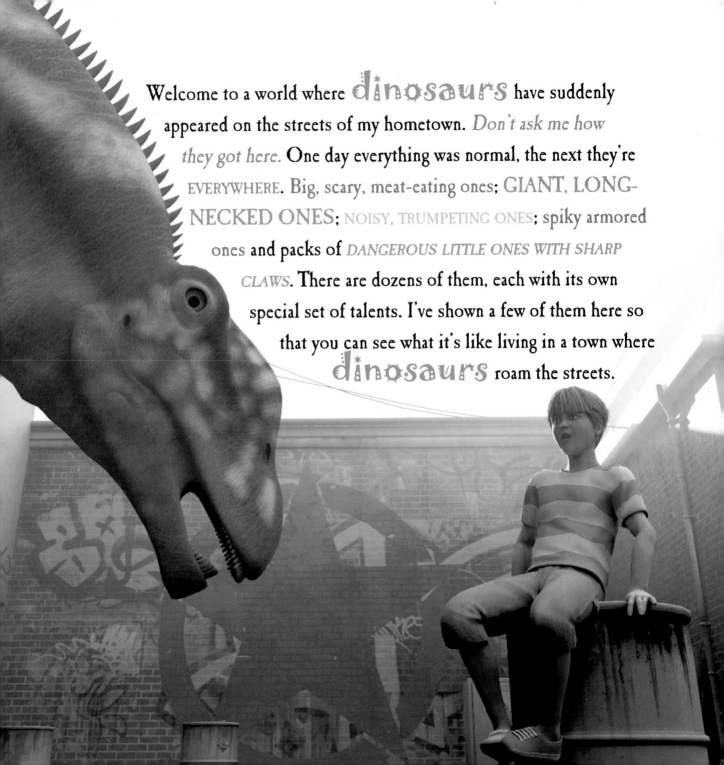

Welcome to a world where dinosaurs have suddenly appeared on the streets of my hometown. *Don't ask me how they got here.* One day everything was normal, the next they're EVERYWHERE. Big, scary, meat-eating ones; GIANT, LONG-NECKED ONES; NOISY, TRUMPETING ONES; spiky armored ones and packs of *DANGEROUS LITTLE ONES WITH SHARP CLAWS.* There are dozens of them, each with its own special set of talents. I've shown a few of them here so that you can see what it's like living in a town where dinosaurs roam the streets.

Altirhinus

al-tih-RYE-nus

This strange-looking dinosaur has a nose that it can blow up like a balloon. It does this to attract female Altirhinuses. It can walk on either two or four legs and has thumb spikes to defend itself from predators.

Altirhinus can grow up to 21 feet (6.5 meters).

Allosaurus

AL-uh-SAWR-us

Driving through the streets early in the morning, you might be lucky enough to see a group of young Allosauruses. They always hunt in packs, running down their prey on their swift and powerful legs.

Allosaurus can grow up to 39 feet (12 meters).

Ankylosaurus

ang-KILE-uh-SAWR-us

An Ankylosaurus wanders through a street that is being demolished. Its tail ends in a club that can smash down walls. Its thick skin is covered in bony lumps from its head to the tip of its tail.

Ankylosaurus can grow up to 23 feet (7 meters).

Argentinosaurus

AHR-gen-TEEN-uh-SAWR-us

In the quieter parts of town you may discover a dinosaur nest. Despite its huge size, Argentinosaurus lays eggs about the size of a soccer ball. Its young take about 40 years to reach adult size.

Argentinosaurus can grow up to 115 feet (35 meters).

Brachiosaurus

BRACK-ee-uh-SAWR-us

Brachiosaurus needs to eat more than 400 pounds (181 kilograms) of food per day. Standing on its back legs it can reach plants high up on the roof gardens of some of the city's tallest apartment buildings.

Brachiosaurus can grow up to 85 feet (26 meters).

Carnotaurus

kahrn-uh-TAWR-us

With a name that means "meat-eating bull," this horned dinosaur has a wicked temper. Watch out if you are wearing red! Even red cars aren't safe when this beast is prowling the streets.

Carnotaurus can grow up to 26 feet (8 meters).

Cryolophosaurus

cry-o-loaf-oh-SAWR-us

Formerly known as Elvisaurus due to its pompadour-like crest, this predator can be seen browsing the stores on the shady side of the street. It comes from Antarctica and is not used to hot weather.

Cryolophosaurus can grow up to 26 feet (8 meters).

Deinonychus

dye-NON-ik-us

Deinonychus has big hands with sharp claws to hold on to its prey. On each foot it has a large curved claw to stab its victims. It keeps this claw off the ground when it moves so it doesn't get blunt.

Deinonychus can grow up to 11 feet (3.5 meters) long.

Deltadromeus

DEL-tah-DROM-ee-us

Down at the beach things can get lively. This speedy predator often hides in the shadows of the pier. When a flying reptile lands on the sand nearby it rushes out to catch it.

Deltadromeus can grow up to 26 feet (8 meters).

Dilophosaurus

dye-LO-fuh-SAWR-us

Watch out for this scary hunter. It has jaws similar to those of a crocodile. It will ambush its prey and use its large clawed hands to grasp it. Its most distinctive feature is the double crest on its head.

Dilophosaurus can grow up to 20 feet (6 meters).

Diplodocus

dih-PLOD-uh-kus

A lone Diplodocus has wandered onto a side street and now has its tail tangled up in overhead cables. These dinosaurs have the longest tails of all. They use them as a whip to scare away meat eaters.

Diplodocus can grow up to 115 feet (35 meters).

Europasaurus

yoo-ROH-pah-SAWR-us

Not all long-necked dinosaurs are huge. These Europasauruses out walking the street look as if they are youngsters. They are actually fully-grown members of a dwarf species related to Brachiosaurus.

Europasaurus can grow up to 20 feet (6 meters).

Giganotosaurus

gig-an-OH-toe-SAWR-us

When riding your bike through the side streets, keep a wary eye out for this gigantic meat eater. At a massive 17,640 pounds (8,000 kilograms) it will crush most things in its path, including cars.

Giganotosaurus can grow up to 43 feet (13 meters).

Gigantoraptor

gee-gan-toe-RAP-tor

Watch out for this giant, feathered hunter. It can run very fast. Unlike true raptors like Velociraptor it does not have a large claw on each foot. It eats mainly plants but also likes an occasional snack of meat.

Gigantoraptor can grow up to 26 feet (8 meters).

Maiasaura

mah-ee-ah-SAWR-uh

In the quieter parts of town you might be lucky enough to come across a nesting site. Maiasauras are good parents. This one is looking after its babies. It made a nest for them in an old tire.

Maiasaura can grow up to 30 feet (9 meters).

Microraptor

my-kro-RAP-tor

Three small dinosaurs glide past a child's window. They have leapt from a tree, scaring away a pair of birds. They use the long feathers on their arms and legs to glide over long distances.

Microraptor can grow up to 2.5 feet (0.8 meters).

Olorotitan

oh-low-ro-ti-tan

Shoppers wearing fashionable hats should beware this duckbilled dinosaur. When a male's crest is brightly colored it is looking for a mate. Colorful hats could be mistaken for a rival's crest.

Olorotitan can grow up to 39 feet (12 meters).

Omeisaurus

Some dinosaurs, like Omeisaurus, have exceptionally long necks. This means they can reach food that other dinosaurs can't, and so get first choice of a basket of fruit, five stories high.

Omeisaurus can grow up to 50 feet (15 meters).

39

Parasaurolophus

A Parasaurolophus sings along with a nearby trumpet player. Its large crest is filled with hollow tubes. It uses them just like the tubes on a trumpet to make its own type of music.

Parasaurolophus can grow up to 36 feet (11 meters).

40

Protoceratops

These small, frilled dinosaurs hang out on the beach where they can dig holes in the sand to bury their eggs. They live in large herds and are very inquisitive and playful, especially with beach balls.

Protoceratops can grow up to 6 feet (1.8 meters).

Spinosaurus

SPY-nuh-SAWR-us

On a hot summer's day, a huge Spinosaurus plods down the street. It doesn't mind the heat. The fin on its back helps to keep it cool. It works like the radiator in a car.

Spinosaurus can grow up to 59 feet (18 meters) long.

Stegosaurus

The petal-shaped plates of Stegosaurus grow from the skin on its back. They also work like a car's radiator. The warm blood running through its plates sends heat into the colder air, and so keeps it cool.

Stegosaurus can grow up to 30 feet (9 meters).

Suchomimus

su-ko-MIE-mus

Take a trip to the park and you might come across this spiky dinosaur wading in the pond. It is looking for its favorite food – fish! Its crocodile-like snout is full of sharp, pointy teeth.

Suchomimus can grow up to 36 feet (11 meters).

Tarbosaurus

TAR-bo-SAWR-us

Sometimes you will see this hungry dinosaur going through the garbage cans. As well as being good hunters these meat eaters are also great scavengers, eating up the scraps of animals that are already dead.

Tarbosaurus can grow up to 33 feet (10 meters).

Torosaurus

A giant among the frilled and horned dinosaurs, Torosaurus is a powerful animal that weighs in at 13,200 pounds (6,000 kilograms). With its massive horns it is used to getting its own way, even when its path is blocked.

Torosaurus can grow up to 25 feet (7.5 meters).

Triceratops

try-SAIR-uh-tops

Its name means "Three-Horned Face" and it is the best known of the frilled and horned dinosaurs. Weighing up to 12,125 pounds (5,500 kilograms), it needs huge amounts of vegetation to keep its hunger satisfied.

Triceratops can grow up to 30 feet (9 meters).

Tyrannosaurus

tie-RAN-oh-SORE-us

In the early evening you might even catch a rare glimpse of this famous dinosaur. At a street crossing in town a mother keeps a close eye on her youngsters.

Tyrannosaurus can grow up to 42 feet (13 meters).

Utahraptor

yoo-tah-RAP-tor

Running along a road, a Utahraptor towers above the people on the pavement. This massive raptor has claws on its feet that can be 8.7 inches (22 centimeters) long. It uses them like a knife to stab its prey.

Utahraptor can grow up to 23 feet (7 meters).

Velociraptor

Four Velociraptors are running off with the boys' soccer ball. Their name means "speedy thief." Just like the larger Deinonychus they are covered in feathers and have a large curved claw on each foot.

Velociraptor can grow up to 6 feet (1.8 meters).

Zuniceratops

zoo-nee-SAIR-uh-tops

In quieter parts of the city you might find a dinosaur's nest. Like all dinosaur mothers this one has laid a clutch of eggs. She will stay close to the nest now and wait for the eggs to hatch.

Zuniceratops can grow up to 10 feet (3 meters).

	Length	Height	Weight	Diet	When it lived	Found in
Altirhinus	21 ft (6.5 m)	6.5 ft (2 m)	8,000 lb (3,630 kg)		Early Cretaceous (144–99 million years ago)	Mongolia
Allosaurus	39 ft (12 m)	16 ft (5 m)	4,410 lb (2,000 kg)		Late Jurassic (159–144 million years ago)	Tanzania, USA
Ankylosaurus	23 ft (7 m)	8 ft (2.5 m)	8,820 lb–15,432 lb (4,000 kg–7,000 kg)		Late Cretaceous (98–65 million years ago)	Canada, USA
Argentinosaurus	115 ft (35 m)	23 ft (7 m)	154,320 lb (70,000 kg)		Late Cretaceous (98–65 million years ago)	Argentina
Brachiosaurus	85 ft (26 m)	41 ft (12.6 m)	154,320 lb (70,000 kg)		Late Jurassic (159–144 million years ago)	Tanzania, USA, Portugal, Algeria
Carnotaurus	26 ft (8 m)	10 ft (3 m)	2,976 lb (1,350 kg)		Late Cretaceous (98–65 million years ago)	Argentina
Cryolophosaurus	26 ft (8 m)	10 ft (3 m)	1,100 lb (500 kg)		Early Jurassic (205–180 million years ago)	Antarctica
Deinonychus	11 ft (3.5 m)	5 ft (1.5 m)	165 lb (75 kg)		Early Cretaceous (144–99 million years ago)	USA
Deltadromeus	26 ft (8 m)	8 ft (2.5 m)	5,512 lb (2,500 kg)		Late Cretaceous (98–65 million years ago)	Morocco
Dilophosaurus	20 ft (6 m)	6.5 ft (2 m)	660 lb–992 lb (300 kg–450 kg)		Early Jurassic (205–180 million years ago)	USA
Diplodocus	115 ft (35 m)	26 ft (8 m)	44,090 lb–55,115 lb (20,000 kg–25,000 kg)		Late Jurassic (159–144 million years ago)	USA
Europasaurus	20 ft (6 m)	10 ft (3 m)	5,997 lb (2,720 kg)		Late Jurassic (159–144 million years ago)	Germany
Giganotosaurus	43 ft (13 m)	16 ft (5 m)	17,640 lb (8,000 kg)		Early Cretaceous (144–99 million years ago)	Argentina
Gigantoraptor	26 ft (8 m)	11 ft (3.5 m)	3,086 lb (1,400 kg)		Late Cretaceous (98–65 million years ago)	Mongolia
Maiasaura	30 ft (9 m)	8.2 ft (2.5 m)	5,511 lb (2,500 kg)		Late Cretaceous (98–65 million years ago)	USA